From
My Heart
to Yours

CONNIE LYNNE ELLIOTT

From My Heart to Yours

Trilogy Christian Publishers
A Wholly Owned Subsidiary of Trinity Broadcasting Network
2442 Michelle Drive Tustin, CA 92780

Manufactured in the United States of America
10 9 8 7 6 5 4 3 2 1
Library of Congress Cataloging-in-Publication Data is available.

ISBN: 978-1-68556-310-3
E-ISBN: 978-1-68556-311-0

DEDICATION

This book is dedicated to my Heavenly Father. He has shown me through the years how a father should love and treat his children. Our relationship has grown and matured over the years as I have spent time in God's presence worshipping, fellowshipping, and reading His Word. He is my secret place. Through His love, I have found trust, safety, peace, security, and confidence in Him.

ACKNOWLEDGMENTS

I would like to acknowledge my husband, Les, who has been the most amazing father to our five children, Brandon, Joshua, Keirsha, Nathaniel, and Jonathan Elliott. I have never known a man to be so calm, patient, loving, and laid back in every season of life. No matter what storms may have come in life, I may have been the wave splashing around, but Les was the stable one to keep the calmness and know the direction of the wind. He is the anchor, love, wisdom, and stability in our marriage and family.

TABLE OF CONTENTS

PREFACE

From My Heart to Yours will encourage and inspire you to cultivate a deeper, loving, and more intimate relationship with your Heavenly Father. We live in a world of deceit and destruction that is targeting the family unit and the relationship that occurs between family members when they spend time with one another. Unfortunately, many people are walking around with a heart full of grief, hurt, bitterness, and anger. They may have come from a broken family or have been hurt by their parents, grandparents, or other loved ones. When this happens, it affects how a relationship is developed between a parent and child, thereby affecting how they develop a relationship with God, their Heavenly Father.

From My Heart to Yours will give you a greater understanding of how much your Heavenly Father loves you so that you can be content, stable, and steadfast in His love. Having a loving, healthy relationship with your Heavenly Father is vitally important in how we live, thrive, and function in life and with our earthly family. It is my earnest desire that through the reading of this book, you obtain a more intimate relationship with your Heavenly Father and comprehend how much He loves you. I pray that through His love, you find completeness in Him.

INTRODUCTION

I finished writing my second book, *Inspirational Messages for Daily Encouragement*, on December 19, 2020, and passed the manuscript off to my husband for him to review. It was an exciting time as God helped me complete a second manuscript by the end of the year 2020. My husband and I took a break to enjoy Christmas with our family, celebrating the birth of Jesus Christ. After Christmas, on the 26th, I began to seek God's direction for 2021 and was just reminiscing of all the wondrous things He did for my husband, me, and my family during the year. I began to brainstorm and dream while writing down what came to me. Before I knew it, I had a whole list written down, and I quietly laid my head on my desk in my office and told God, "I am going to just seek You, and You will help me bring everything to pass that needs to be completed for Your glory." It felt amazing as I just released it over to God. The very next day, on December 27, 2020, at 3:30 p.m. in the afternoon, while walking through my bathroom, I heard the words, "From My Heart to Yours," and I felt a gush of wind hit my spirit. At that moment, a knowing came to me—that was the name of my next book. I was so excited, I quickly went to my office and wrote the name of my third book down on paper and any other thoughts as I was led by the Spirit of God.

As you read this book, I believe our Heavenly Father wants you to know who He is and understand how much He loves you. *From My Heart to Yours* is a book where God desires to share *the love of the Father* in a whole new perspective. Pour yourself a cup of tea (or coffee), sit back, relax, and learn about your Heavenly Father and allow Him to speak His unconditional love into your life through the words on each page of this book.

About the Book Cover

When the name of this book was dropped into my spirit, I visually saw a picture of a hand coming down from heaven at the same time as I was reaching up to heaven. Our two hands met, and we clasped hands tightly. I knew that an exchange of love, trust, and protection had occurred between my Heavenly Father and me. I described what I visually saw in the picture to one of my sons, and he shared with me two scriptures that confirmed the picture. I was comforted when I read the words found in Isaiah 41:10 (NIV). It says, "…for I am your God. I will strengthen you and help you; I will uphold you with my righteous right hand." "For I hold you by your right hand—I, the LORD your God. And I say to you, 'Don't be afraid. I am here to help you'" (Isaiah 41:13, NLT). We are never alone. God is here to help each one of us because He loves us.

CHAPTER 1

In the Beginning

Have you ever thought about the words "in the beginning"? A book has a beginning and an end. A race has a beginning and end. Your life has a beginning and an end. So what does this all mean, and how does it apply in the grand scheme of life in a relationship with God, your Heavenly Father? In this chapter, we will go to a passage found in Genesis so you can have a greater understanding of who God is and what He has done for you.

Genesis 1:1 (NIV) says, "In the beginning God created the heavens and the earth." God created everything, and when He saw the entirety of what was made, He was pleased and said in verse 31 (NIV), "…it was very good." So you might ask, "What did God create?" Let's review the days of creation in the following table that summarizes Genesis 1:1–31.

Day 1	God created light and darkness, day and night.
Day 2	God created a space between waters to separate water from heaven and water from earth. The space was called sky.
Day 3	God created land and seas. The land produced vegetation.

Day 4	God created the sun, moon, and stars.
Day 5	God created the living creatures of the seas and birds to fly in the sky.
Day 6	God made living creatures of the land. He then created man (both male and female) in the likeness of Him to rule over the fish in the seas and the birds in the sky, over the livestock and all the wild animals, and over all the creatures that move along the ground.
Day 7	God rested.

You can see that in the first six days, God created and formed the environment and everything that we could imagine to see in the sky, on land, or under the sea. After all that was prepared, He made man and woman, blessed them, and told them to be fruitful and increase in number, fill the earth and subdue it. God made the entirety for us to enjoy and provided everything to meet all of our needs.

Let's reminisce and look at an example. Remember back to when you and your spouse (friend, relative, etc.) found out you were expecting a baby and you were going to be a father/mother (aunt/uncle, etc.). You were so excited and full of emotions. You found yourself looking around your environment and analyzing everything you had in preparation for this new baby. The clock is ticking! You have nine months to get everything perfectly cleaned up, organized, and prepared so you can bring home your new baby. As you lovingly care for your baby and he/she grows, develops, and matures, you set boundaries and rules for the safety and protection of your child.

That same holds true to God. That is what He did for us. He spent the first six days of creation preparing everything in the environment so that when He made man and woman, He was able to place them in the middle of all His glorious creation to enjoy, increase in number, rule, and fellowship with God. He, too, just as the parents of the child, set boundaries for the protection of mankind.

Names of God

As you look around and see the beauty of God's creation and all that was made for mankind, you may ask yourself, *Who is this God?* It says in Exodus 3:10 that God told Moses He was sending him to Pharaoh to bring the Israelites out of Egypt. In verses 11–15 (NIV), it goes on to say:

> But Moses said to God, "Who am I that I should go to Pharaoh and bring the Israelites out of Egypt?" And God said, "I will be with you. And this will be the sign to you that it is I who have sent you: When you have brought the people out of Egypt, you will worship God on this mountain." Moses said to God, "Suppose I go to the Israelites and say to them, 'The God of your fathers has sent me to you,' and they ask me, 'What is his name?' Then what shall I tell them?" God said to Moses, "I AM WHO I AM. This is what you are to say to the Israelites: 'I AM has sent me to you.'" God also said to Moses, "Say to the Israelites, 'The LORD, the God of your fathers—the God of Abraham, the God of Isaac and the God of

Jacob—has sent me to you.' This is my name forever, the name you shall call me from generation to generation."

Through this story, God tells Moses that He is the God whose name is I AM WHO I AM. This was not meant for only Moses and the Israelites but for generation to generation. That includes you, your children, your grandchildren, your great-grandchildren, and generations to follow.

I AM WHO I AM is not the only name that God is known by, so I would like to review a few of the other wonderful names of God. Keep in mind that every name is in reverence to God and what He can provide for you. The following names of God can be seen in a beautiful video with music that I would encourage you to watch. It has a lovely melody that will touch your heart and lead you right into worshiping God.[1] I have also included the scripture reference for your review.

NAME	DEFINITION	BIBLE REF.
Elohim	The all-powerful One, Creator.	Genesis 1:1
Jehovah-Shammah	The Lord is there; the Lord, my companion.	Ezekiel 48:35
Adonai	The Lord, my Great Lord.	Genesis 15:2
El Elyon	The God Most High.	Genesis 14:18
Yhwh	"I AM," the One who is the self-existent One.	Exodus 3:14

---

1   Denison, 2018

Jehovah-Rohi	The Lord is my Shepherd.	Psalm 23:1
Jehovah-Mekaddishkem	The Lord who sanctifies.	Exodus 31:13
Jehovah-Tsidkenu	The Lord, our righteousness.	Jeremiah 23:6
El Roi	The God who sees me.	Genesis 16:13
Jehovah-Nissi	The Lord is my banner.	Exodus 17:15
El Shaddai	The all-sufficient One, the God of the mountains, God Almighty.	Genesis 17:1
Jehovah-Jireh	The Lord will provide.	Genesis 22:14
Jehovah-Rapha	The Lord who heals.	Exodus 15:26
Jehovah-Shalom	The Lord is peace.	Judges 6:24
Jehovah-Sabaoth	The Lord of hosts, the Lord of armies.	1 Samuel 1:3
El Olam	The eternal God, the everlasting God.	Genesis 21:33
El Elohe Yisrael	God, the God of Israel.	Genesis 33:20
Immanuel	God with us, "I AM."	Isaiah 7:14
Yah or Jah	"I AM," the One who is the self-existent One.	Psalm 68:4
Jehovah	"I AM," the One who is the self-existent One.	Genesis 2:4

When you read all the different names of God and their definitions, you realize that the God we serve is a magnificent God. It says in Psalm 145:1–6 (MSG):

> I lift you high in praise, my God, O my King! And I'll bless your name into eternity. I'll bless you every day, and keep it up from now to eternity. God is magnificent; he can never be praised enough. There are no boundaries to his greatness. Generation after generation stands in awe of your work; each one tells stories of your mighty acts. Your beauty and splendor have everyone talking; I compose songs on your wonders. Your marvelous doings are headline news; I could write a book full of the details of your greatness.

Those scriptures tell it perfectly that you and I can speak about the goodness of God all the days of our life and pass it down from one generation to another.

Characteristics of God

Have you ever thought about what God is like and who He is? If you were to describe the characteristics of your natural father, what would you say? Would you describe features like his height, weight, physique, hair, and other features? Characteristics are defined by the distinguishing qualities, attributes, or traits of a person.[2] The Bible reveals the characteristics of God, and they are listed in the table below. As you dive into the following scrip-

---

2   Dictionary.com, 2021

tures, you will discover and identify these traits that our Heavenly Father God possesses.

God is holy.	1 Samuel 2:2, Revelations 4:8
God is Spirit.	John 4:24
God is infinite (endless, immeasurable).	Colossians 1:17
God is immutable (absolute, complete).	Malachi 3:6
God is self-sufficient.	John 5:26
God is omnipotent (all-mighty, all-powerful).	Psalm 33:6
God is omniscient (all-knowing, all-seeing).	Isaiah 46:9–10
God is omnipresent (ever-present; God is everywhere).	Psalm 139:7–10
God is wise.	Romans 11:33
God is loving.	1 John 3:1, 1 John 4:7–8
God is faithful and righteous.	Deuteronomy 7:9, Psalm 145:17
God is powerful and mighty.	Psalm 24:8
God is sovereign (supreme) and just.	Deuteronomy 32:4, Psalm 103:19
God is compassionate and gracious.	Psalm 103:8, Psalm 145:8
God is glorious.	Psalm 72:19, Habakkuk 3:4
God is good.	Psalm 34:8

God is forgiving and merciful.	Romans 9:15–16, 1 John 1:9
God is our refuge (shelter) and help.	Psalm 46:1
God is with us.	Isaiah 41:10
God never changes.	Numbers 23:19, Malachi 3:6, Hebrews 13:8
God is our Father.	Isaiah 64:8; Ephesians 4:6, 1 Corinthians 8:6

What a list of incredible characteristics and traits describing our Heavenly Father God. I pray that your eyes have been enlightened and that you comprehend the magnitude that we have a Father God who is more than enough. He is our all-sufficient Father who desires to have every one of your needs met, whether it be mentally, physically, emotionally, or spiritually. It says in 2 Corinthians 9:8 (ESV), "And God is able to make all grace abound to you, so that having all sufficiency in all things at all times, you may abound in every good work."

The Godhead

We can't leave this chapter without talking about the Godhead. Some may refer to the Godhead as the Trinity, but the actual word "Trinity" is not found in the Bible. The one and true God is composed of God the Father, God the Son, and God the Holy Spirit. All three make up the Godhead. The following scriptures have been provided from the Word of God to help you understand the completeness of Godhead and to absorb and comprehend this information. As you read through these scriptures, you will notice the distinctions of the Godhead.

> And when Jesus was baptized, immediately he went up from the water, and behold, the heavens were opened to him, and he saw the Spirit of God descending like a dove and coming to rest on him; and behold, a voice from heaven said, "This is my beloved Son, with whom I am well pleased."
>
> — Matthew 3:16–17 (ESV)

> In the beginning was the Word, and the Word was with God, and the Word was God. He was with God in the beginning. Through him all things were made; without him nothing was made that has been made. In him was life, and that life was the light of all mankind. The light shines in the darkness, and the darkness has not overcome it.
>
> — John 1:1–5 (NIV)

> The Word became flesh and made his dwelling among us. We have seen his glory, the glory of the one and only Son, who came from the Father, full of grace and truth.
>
> — John 1:14 (NIV)

> But the Helper (Comforter, Advocate, Intercessor— Counselor, Strengthener, Standby), the Holy Spirit,

whom the Father will send in My name [in My place, to represent Me and act on My behalf], He will teach you all things. And He will help you remember everything that I have told you.

— John 14:26 (AMP)

But for us, There is one God, the Father, by whom all things were created, and for whom we live. And there is one Lord, Jesus Christ, through whom all things were created, and through whom we live.

— First Corinthians 8:6 (NLT)

For in Him all the fullness of Deity (the Godhead) dwells in bodily form [completely expressing the divine essence of God].

— Colossians 2:9 (AMP)

We proclaim to you the one who existed from the beginning, whom we have heard and seen. We saw him with our own eyes and touched him with our own hands. He is the Word of life. This one who is life itself was revealed to us, and we have seen him. And now we testify and proclaim to you that he is the one who is eternal life. He was with the Father, and then he was revealed to us.

— First John 1:1–2 (NLT)

For there are three that bear witness in heaven: the Father, the Word, and the Holy Spirit; and these three are one. And there are three that bear witness on earth: the Spirit, the water, and the blood; and these three agree as one.

— First John 5:7–8 (NKJV)

Now, let's look at an example of an object lesson that you can complete to help you comprehend the complexity of the Godhead. Ready for some fun! Place a solid ice cube in a pan on the stove. The solid cube represents God the Father. As the cube melts and is heated, it turns into steam. As the steam rises, it represents God the Holy Spirit. The water that remains in the pan represents God the Son (Jesus). Through the one ice cube, three elements are displayed. The water, the ice, and the steam are each unique and distinct, but they are also all exactly the same. In a similar way, God the Father, God the Son, and God the Holy Spirit are unique and distinct but are one.[3]

As we end this chapter, I hope you have a clearer understanding of the creation of God, who God is, what kind of characteristics God possesses, and the distinction of the Godhead. I have listed below a few more scriptures that speak of the Godhead from the Word of God.

For a child is born to us, a son is given to us. The government will rest on his shoulders. And he will be called: Wonderful Counselor, Mighty God, Everlasting Father, Prince of Peace.

— Isaiah 9:6 (NLT)

---

3 Free Bible Lessons, 2021

"Go therefore and make disciples of all nations, baptizing them in the name of the Father and of the Son and of the Holy Spirit."

— Matthew 28:19 (ESV)

The Son radiates God's own glory and expresses the very character of God, and he sustains everything by the mighty power of his command. When he had cleansed us from our sins, he sat down in the place of honor at the right hand of the majestic God in heaven.

— Hebrews 1:3 (NLT)

He also says to the Son, "In the beginning, Lord, you laid the foundation of the earth and made the heavens with your hands."

— Hebrews 1:10 (NLT)

CHAPTER 2

Family Ancestry

As we move into this chapter, think back to when you lived at home with your parents and you had to put together a school project about your family genealogy or ancestry. Where did your family originate from? How far back can you track your ancestry? Did you discover anything exciting or unusual? All these questions are food for thought about where you came from and the history of your family. In the kingdom of God, there is a family ancestry as well. The Holy Bible tells us about the lineage of Jesus, who is the Son of God and born of a virgin woman, Mary, and her husband, Joseph. We can trace back Jesus' lineage to the beginning of mankind when God made Adam.

As a child of God, it is important to understand our lineage. God provided us with the written Word of God so we can get to know Him and understand the family in which we belong to. We find that God chose people throughout history to prepare the way for the salvation of the Lord. Both the book of Matthew 1:1–16 and Luke 3: 34–38 record the genealogy of Jesus Christ, who was the descendant of David, Abraham, and Adam, the first man of creation. The following list has been compiled to show the lineage back to God.

- Jesus, who was called the Messiah, was born to Mary and her husband, Joseph.

- Jacob was the father of Joseph.

- Matthan, the father of Jacob;

- Eleazar, the father of Matthan;

- Elihud, the father of Eleazar;

- Akim, the father of Elihud;

- Zadok, the father of Akim;

- Azor, the father of Zadok;

- Eliakim, the father of Azor;

- Abihud, the father of Eliakim;

- Zerubbabel, the father of Abihud;

- Shealtiel, the father of Zerubbabel;

- Jeconiah was the father of Shealtiel;

- Josiah, the father of Jeconiah;

- Amon, the father of Josiah;

- Manasseh, the father of Amon;

- Hezekiah, the father of Manasseh;

- Ahaz, the father of Hezekiah;

- Jotham, the father of Ahaz;

- Uzziah, the father of Jotham;

- Jehoram, the father of Uzziah;

From My Heart to Yours

- Jehoshaphat, the father of Jehoram;

- Asa, the father of Jehoshaphat;

- Abijah, the father of Asa;

- Rehoboam, the father of Abijah;

- Solomon, the father of Rehoboam;

- David was the father of Solomon;

- Jesse, the father of King David;

- Obed, the father of Jesse;

- Boaz, the father of Obed;

- Salmon, the father of Boaz;

- Nahshon, the father of Salmon;

- Amminadab, the father of Nahshon;

- Ram, the father of Amminadab;

- Hezron, the father of Ram;

- Perez, the father of Hezron;

- Judah, the father of Perez and Zerah;

- Jacob, the father of Judah and his brothers;

- Isaac, the father of Jacob;

- Abraham was the father of Isaac;

- Terah was the father of Abraham;

- Nahor was the father of Terah;

- Serug was the father of Nahor;

- Reu was the father of Serug;

- Peleg was the father of Reu;

- Eber was the father of Peleg;

- Shelah was the father of Eber;

- Cainan was the father of Shelah;

- Arphaxad was the father of Cainan;

- Shem was the father of Arphaxad;

- Noah was the father of Shem;

- Lamech was the father of Noah;

- Methuselah was the father of Lamech;

- Enoch was the father of Methuselah;

- Jared was the father of Enoch;

- Mahalalel was the father of Jared;

- Kenan was the father of Mahalalel;

- Enosh was the father of Kenan;

- Seth was the father of Enosh;

- Adam was the father of Seth;

- God was the father of Adam, the firstborn of creation.

The family tree presented above tells the story of God's faithfulness from generation to generation through the birth of Jesus. Jesus was born into this world to restore the relationship between God and mankind that had originally been created before deceit entered into the heart of man/woman. When Jesus entered His ministry at the age of thirty, He went around teaching and preaching about the kingdom of God and healed people who had faith to receive it until He was taken up to heaven to sit at the right hand of God (Mark 16:19).

Holy Spirit

The Holy Spirit was given to us by God when Jesus returned to heaven to be at the right hand of the Father (Ephesians 1:20–23; Mark 16:19). In Acts 1:4–8 (NIV), Jesus commanded the apostles before He left to:

> "…not leave Jerusalem, but wait for the gift my Father promised, which you have heard me speak about. For John baptized with water, but in a few days you will be baptized with the Holy Spirit." Then they gathered around him and asked him, "Lord, are you at this time going to restore the kingdom to Israel?" He said to them: "It is not for you to know the times or dates the Father has set by his own authority. But you will receive power when the Holy Spirit comes on you; and you will be my witnesses in Jerusalem, and in all Judea and Samaria, and to the ends of the earth."

The apostles joined their fellow believers in the upper room in Jerusalem.

> When the day of Pentecost came, they were all together in one place. Suddenly a sound like the

blowing of a violent wind came from heaven and filled the whole house where they were sitting. They saw what seemed to be tongues of fire that separated and came to rest on each of them. All of them were filled with the Holy Spirit and began to speak in other tongues as the Spirit enabled them.

— Acts 2:1–4 (NIV)

When the people who spoke in other tongues were accused of being drunk by the Jews, Peter stood up and made the following announcement, which is found in Acts 2:17–21 (ESV):

And in the last days it shall be, God declares, that I will pour out my Spirit on all flesh and your sons and your daughters shall prophesy, and your young men shall see visions, and your old men shall dream dreams; even on my male servants and female servants in those days I will pour out my Spirit, and they shall prophesy. And I will show wonders in the heavens above and signs on the earth below, blood, and fire, and vapor of smoke; the sun shall be turned to darkness and the moon to blood, before the day of the Lord comes, the great and magnificent day. And it shall come to pass that everyone who calls upon the name of the Lord shall be saved.

And then, in verse 38 (ESV), it says, "And Peter said to them, 'Repent and be baptized every one of you in the name of Jesus Christ for the forgiveness of your sins, and you will receive the gift of the Holy Spirit.'" As we call upon the name of the Lord, we shall be saved. When that happens, the indwelling of the Holy

Spirit occurs; John 16:13 (ESV) says, "When the Spirit of truth comes, he will guide you into all the truth, for he will not speak on his own authority, but whatever he hears he will speak, and he will declare to you the things that are to come." It also says in John 14:26 (ESV), "But the Helper, the Holy Spirit, whom the Father will send in my name, he will teach you all things and bring to your remembrance all that I have said to you."

Both our Heavenly Father and Jesus knew that we needed the Holy Spirit to live our life as children of God in this earth. He was given to us to be our support system. The Holy Spirit plays a significant role in our life by leading us into truth, encouraging us, convicting us, comforting us, sanctifying us, purifying us, being our helper, and praying the perfect will of God for our life. It is imperative to understand the difference between conviction and condemnation. Romans 8:1 (NIV) says, "Therefore, there is now no condemnation for those who are in Christ Jesus." It also says in John 3:17 (ESV), "For God did not send his Son into the world to condemn the world, but in order that the world might be saved through him."

An article written by Mark Ballenger (2017) said conviction leads to life, and condemnation leads to death. He further expounded by saying:

> One main difference between condemnation and conviction is where they will lead you. Condemnation leads you further away from God towards death. Conviction leads you closer to God and towards life.
>
> Biblical condemnation is more than a feeling. It is a state of being that defines your relationship with God. When you stand before God condemned, it means your current eternal home is away from God

in hell. To be condemned means you have been found guilty and have been sentenced to death.

Conviction, on the other hand, is when our wrongs have been identified and revealed. The Bible explains that Christians can be convicted of sin while not condemned. We can be found guilty of sin and yet not be sentenced to the just judgment for those sins.

In love, God makes Christians aware of sin (conviction) without giving us the sentence (condemnation) for that sin. He sent his Holy Spirit to bring conviction and to allow humans to escape condemnation. God doesn't just remove the penalty of our sins without bringing conviction. Rather, through a loving conviction of sin God draws us to himself, causes us to repent, and leads us towards life.

Whatever your circumstances in life may be, remember God is here to help you. He will never leave you nor forsake you (Hebrews 13:5). In understanding the purpose of the Holy Spirit, we can trust and allow Him to move in our life so the fruits of the Spirit can be manifested. Our life should reveal love, joy, peace, longsuffering, gentleness, goodness, faith, meekness, and temperance (Galatians 5:22–23). This is our witness to the world that we can walk out our life with the power of the Holy Spirit, which Jesus promised us when He ascended into heaven to be at the right hand of the Father (Acts 1:8–9).

CHAPTER 3

Who's Your Daddy?

I want you to think back to the earliest years of your life. For some of you, you may remember glimpses at the age of four and some, the age of eight. Whatever the age may be, now think about the relationship that you had with your father. The emotions you may be experiencing right now may trigger anger and sadness or love and happiness as you recall events that occurred in your life as a child. Every person is going to answer these questions differently based on how you were raised and the relationship you had with your father. Maybe you knew about your father but did not know him personally. Maybe you did not know your father at all, and your mother or grandparents raised you. Maybe you were adopted and did not know your biological father but had a great relationship with the father who adopted you. Maybe you had a wonderful father, and when you think about him, it brings you great love and comfort that he was supportive and good to you all the days of your growing up years. He was your hero, and you hoped and prayed that someday you could be just like him.

If any of you know me personally, you know that I talk about the goodness of God and how He is faithful. I know that God loves me. He cares for me, supports me, encourages me, and corrects me. I find security, confidence, and trust in God because I know that God is always with me. I have an intimate relationship with God because I spend time getting to know Him through prayer, worship, and reading His Word. We have a love song, and every day when I am seeking God in the morning, I tell Him, "It's time for our song." I play it and just worship God as I sing to Him and soak in the presence of God.

The relationship that I have with God did not happen overnight, but rather it has taken years, as I have spent time in His presence getting to know Him on a daily basis. I would like to share with you some stories from my childhood to show the love, grace, mercy, and goodness of God. These stories are not shared in disrespect to my parents but rather to let you know that whatever your situation may have been growing up or that you are in right now, God will make a way. Romans 8:28 (NIV) says, "And we know that in all things God works for the good of those who love Him, who have been called according to his purpose." That scripture alone is reassuring to know that life can be victorious and rewarding if we just fix our eyes on God and trust in Him that everything is going to be all right. When we trust God, we have security and confidence.

I grew up in the Midwest. I lived in a large family of seven that included my parents, two sisters, and two brothers. It was not the perfect family by any means, but my parents did the very best they could within their means. The living environment was not the healthiest. It was tough and challenging. My dad was an alcoholic. He drank all the time and oftentimes gambled away his money. He was abusive physically, emotionally, and sexually. My mother worked hard to provide for the family, keep a roof over our heads and food on the table.

Unfortunately, the family environment shaped me into a strong and independent child where my first response to anything was to stand up and fight. I always laughed, was sociable, and appeared happy, but deep down, I was sad, hurting, and lonely. Anyone that knew our family would have never suspected any of this. My parents were well-liked people, and they were involved in different community activities.

I desperately needed a way out, but as a child, I had nowhere to go. My way out was sitting on the floor in my bedroom closet by myself. I would talk to God and read the Bible using a flashlight. Why a flashlight, you ask? Because it was dark and there were no lights in the closet. I was told there was a God, and I had accepted Jesus Christ as my Lord and Savior at the age of seven, but I did not, in my eyes, have a relationship with God. I just hoped and believed that if I read the Bible enough, God would hear me and help me.

When Life Throws a Curveball

At the age of twelve, I was walking down the hallway in the doublewide trailer that my family lived in, and I remember my mother stopping me to tell me, "If a man stops you and tells you he's your father—he probably is." I was shocked and couldn't believe it. The dad that had been raising me for the first twelve years of my life was not my biological father but rather my stepdad. I had his last name, and he was the only dad I ever knew. My older siblings knew about our biological father, but I did not. I was the fourth child in line, and my mother and biological father had separated when she was pregnant with me. My mother remarried when I was one, and there was never any talk in the family about another father. Apparently, my biological father had been looking for us, and at the age of twelve, he finally found out where we lived and contacted my mother and stepdad. I had many questions that ran through my mind. What happened? Who was I? *Why don't I have my biological father's last name? Who is my father? Why is he not in my life? Did he want me?* There were many other questions and emotions that began to stir up within my mind. This was a traumatic time in my life, and I found myself going through an identity crisis and so desperately wanted to know my biological father and be accepted by him.

God Will Make a Way

Through persistence and determination, I was able to finally meet my biological father at the age of thirteen. I met him in a parking lot by the post office of the trailer court that my family lived in. My biological father and his fiancée rolled down the window of their car and spoke to my two sisters and me for about fifteen minutes. They stayed in their car and never got out. As I watched them drive off, little did I realize that it was this encounter that would change my destiny! You see, one reason my biological father wanted to meet me was to find out if I really was his daughter. It didn't take but a few brief moments to erase any doubts of who my real father was by my appearance and nature.

After that day, I thought about my biological father continuously. I couldn't get him out of my mind. He was always on my heart. I went to my older sister and asked her if she could help me see him again. Through conversations back and forth between my older sister and my biological father, my sister was able to arrange a date, time, and place where we could meet again. This was a very risky situation, as my mother and stepdad did not know about the arrangements. It was not an honest decision, but

I knew they would say no if I went up and asked to meet with my biological father.

My sister made the arrangements and planned the whole day so we could spend time with our biological father and get to know him and his fiancée. The meeting date was scheduled for Easter Sunday, so I asked my parents if I could go to church with my sister that day, go out for lunch, and they agreed. So the trip began. My sister and I went to her church that day, where we met up with our biological father and his fiancée. I was excited and scared at the same time because my sister and I were not being honest with our parents and planned the events of the day behind their backs. It was not a good situation to be in, but I had a deep desire to know who my biological father was, and I was willing to take that risk. After church, we all went out for lunch at a really nice restaurant where we just spent more time together talking and getting to know one another.

I have pictures of that day when the four of us stood together side by side, not knowing when we would see each other again. I remember the excitement that I had when my biological father said he had brought me a gift. He gave me a life-size, red, and white teddy bear. I had always wanted a large teddy bear, and my heart was full of joy to receive it.

Time was passing, and it was getting late in the afternoon. We had to get back home, so my sister and I put the teddy bear into the car, and we returned home. I don't recall much of the rest of that day, as it was very traumatic. My parents found out what my sister and I did and that the teddy bear was a gift from my biological father. My stepdad threw the teddy bear outside into the snow. We were not allowed to have anything in the house from my biological father. I cried because that was a gift from my biological father, and it was something that I had always wanted, and it was dear to my heart.

I looked outside at the teddy bear in the snow, and I asked my stepdad if I could give it away. I had his permission, so I went next door where two little girls lived and knocked on their door. I asked their mother if she thought her children would like this life-size teddy bear, and they received it joyfully. I left their home knowing the teddy bear was in a good home and the girls would enjoy it.

Relationship Building

I slowly began developing a relationship with my biological father through my late teenage years, and he started to become a part of my life. When I was in my freshman year finishing up the first semester of college, I was given the opportunity to move in with my biological father and his wife and attend college where they lived. I accepted the offer and moved to their home in December of 1985. It was a long drive from Vermillion, South Dakota, to Marshalltown, Iowa. I remember the day when I arrived to meet my biological father. He was selling Christmas trees in the parking lot of a local restaurant, The Golden Corral. He saw me, greeted me with a hug, and closed up the business for the day. We went inside the restaurant, sat at a table, and visited while he sipped on coffee and I sipped on hot chocolate. The move was not an easy decision to make, but deep down in my heart, I had a knowing and peace that it was the right thing to do.

After the move, I was able to get connected with a church and grow in my relationship with my Heavenly Father and my biological father. We became close, and I was amazed at how much we were alike even though I didn't grow up with him. Many of the questions that I had been thinking about for years were answered, and some things I just had to let go and believe God that whatever happened in the past was the past. I could have become bitter and angry over my past, but that would not have helped me but rather would have hindered my future. I needed to forgive everyone that had hurt me and press into what God had for me and what was in my heart. The Bible says in Isaiah 43:18–19 (ESV), "Remember not the former things, nor consider the things of old. Behold, I am doing a new thing; now it springs forth, do you not perceive it? I will make a way in the wilderness and rivers in the desert." God made a way in my life to meet my biological father and build that relationship with him over time.

A Grandmother's Prayers

It was several years later into my adulthood that I found out my biological father had the opportunity to spend time with me when I was one year old. I was told that my biological father was faced with a decision to take me to meet my paternal grandparents or take me to church and have me dedicated. That day he chose God! He took me to church and had me dedicated to God. I never did get the chance to meet my paternal grandfather before he died, but I did meet my paternal grandmother twice before she died. I found out later in life that she prayed for her other grandchildren and me continuously. I cannot tell you what prayers she prayed, but God honored her prayers, and when I was nineteen years old, I had the opportunity to meet her for the very first time.

Your Heavenly Father

Just as my biological father loved me, prayed for me, and desired to have a relationship with me, you have a Heavenly Father who loves you and desires to have a relationship with you. He wants to bless you with wonderful gifts for no other reason than He loves you. Not only did He create this world that you live in, but He created and formed you in your mother's womb. (Psalm 139:13). You were made in His image (Genesis 1:27), and you have His eyes! He wants to be your Daddy. He has such a desire to have a relationship with you that God sent Jesus to earth to restore your relationship with your Heavenly Father. This was done through the death and resurrection of Jesus Christ, the Son of God.

Will you connect with your Heavenly Father and come home to Him? He is a loving and patient Father who has His arms wide open and stretched towards you. He misses you. It is your choice to have a relationship with your Father God but know that without Him, you will be incomplete. If you choose to cultivate a relationship, not only will you be complete in Him, you fulfill a longing in your Heavenly Father's heart!

CHAPTER 4

I Have Been Adopted

We are surrounded by people every day, and unless someone tells you that they were adopted, you may never know. Families are unique, and every family situation will vary in dynamics. This chapter will give you an understanding of adoption through definitions, personal stories, and biblical stories of men and women found in the Bible.

Definition of Adoption by Law

In order to understand the true meaning of adoption, let's take a look at the definition according to the law. It states, "The act of one who takes another's child into his own family, treating him as his own, and giving him all the rights and duties of his own child. A juridical act creating between two persons certain relations, purely civil, of paternity and filiation."[4] It goes on further to describe that an adoptive parent is a person who "…completes the legal requirements necessary to adopt a child that is not his or her biological child and agrees to accept all the responsibilities for the care of the child as if he or she was the biological parent."[5]

---

4   THELAW.com Dictionary
5   Ib.

In other words, the parent accepts that child as his/her own and enters into an agreed contract by law. The parent takes full responsibility to meet the child's every need financially, emotionally, spiritually, and physically. Dr. Harley Rotbart, a nationally-renowned parenting expert and vice-chair emeritus of pediatrics at Children's Hospital Colorado, says there are eight essential requirements for children to thrive, be happy, and become successful adults. They need security, stability, consistency, emotional support, love, education, positive role models, and structure.[6] The child, once adopted, has full access as a family heir as if the child was born by blood.

Personal Stories

My biological father never relinquished his rights to be my father; therefore, I was never able to be adopted by my stepdad or legally take his name. The only other way the adoption could occur would be when I turned the age of eighteen, and then it would be my choice of who I wanted my legal father to be and what name I chose. Even though I was not legally adopted, I remained under my stepdad's last name until after I graduated from high school. At the age of eighteen, by means of no influence by any person, even though deep in my heart, I had made my decision years previously, I took my birthright name back and went through the process to make all the necessary name changes, and I continued with my birth name until I married my husband and took his last name.

---

6   Rotbart, 2021

When God was talking to me about adoption, He reminded me of people I knew in my life who had been adopted into other families. When I would speak with the children who were adopted, they were so grateful for both their biological parents and their adoptive parents. They knew they were loved by both sets of parents. They had an understanding that their biological parents chose the family they would be placed in, and the family would love them, financially provide for them, and give them an environment to grow, flourish, and thrive in life. Some people may struggle with the fact that they were adopted. They may have many questions about their biological parents and why they were given up for adoption. Hopefully, through the years, the answers were somehow revealed, or you were able to have some form of closure. If you have not received closure, I pray God will bring revelation to your eyes and healing to your heart as you read the words written in this book.

One story that touched my life regarding adoption occurred in my teenage years. I babysat for a family who had two beautiful children who were greatly loved by their parents. I had discovered later on that these children had been adopted into this family when they were babies. The biological mothers were unable to care for their babies and wrote a love letter to them explaining why they were placed up for adoption. The parents who adopted these two children placed the letters in their baby album, and I had the opportunity to read them. It was so beautiful and emotional. I could feel the love in the letters as the biological mothers poured their heart and soul into every word written. Both children knew they were adopted and would tell other people that they were adopted and loved by both their biological mother and adoptive parents.

Adoption into the Kingdom of God

Just as these two children were adopted into their new family, you have been given the opportunity to be adopted into the kingdom of God's family. Ephesians 1:5 (NLT) says, "God decided in advance to adopt us into his own family by bringing us to himself through Jesus Christ. This is what He wanted to do, and it gave Him great pleasure." God has given you the free will to choose what family you want to be a part of. The question is, do you want to choose life everlasting or death and destruction? John 5:24 (NIV) says, "Very truly I tell you, whoever hears my word and believes Him who sent me has eternal life and will not be judged but has crossed over from death to life." Believing in Jesus and accepting Him as your Lord and Savior provide you the right to become a child of God (John 1:12).

The exciting news is when a child is adopted into an earthly family, the father accepts him or her as a son or daughter with full rights to his name and inheritance. When we choose to join the heavenly family, God tells us in 2 Corinthians 6:18 (NLT), "And I will be your Father, and you will be my sons and daughters, says the Lord Almighty." We then take on the name "Christian" with full benefits as a child in the kingdom of God. Through Jesus' birth, death, and resurrection, He made the way for our relationship with God to be restored and acquire sonship. We are entitled to the benefits of His family, which include health, healing, life, prosperity, joy, peace, sanctification, and blessings. I would like to share Psalm 103:1–22 (NIV) to further expound on the benefits of sonship in the kingdom of God:

Praise the Lord, my soul; all my inmost being, praise his holy name. Praise the Lord, my soul, and forget not all his benefits—who forgives all your sins and heals all your diseases, who redeems your life from the pit and crowns you with love and compassion, who satisfies your desires with good things so that your youth is renewed like the eagle's. The Lord works righteousness and justice for all the oppressed. He made known his ways to Moses, his deeds to the people of Israel: The Lord is compassionate and gracious, slow to anger, abounding in love. He will not always accuse, nor will he harbor his anger forever; he does not treat us as our sins deserve or repay us according to our iniquities. For as high as the heavens are above the earth, so great is his love for those who fear him; as far as the east is from the west, so far has he removed our transgressions from us. As a father has compassion on his children, so the Lord has compassion on those who fear him; for he knows how we are formed, he remembers that we are dust. The life of mortals is like grass, they flourish like a flower of the field; the wind blows over it and it is gone, and its place remembers it no more. But from everlasting to everlasting the Lord's love is with those who fear him, and his righteousness with their children's children—with those who keep his covenant and remember to obey his precepts. The Lord has established his throne in heaven, and his kingdom rules over all. Praise the Lord, you his angels, you mighty ones who do his bidding, who obey his word. Praise the Lord, all his heavenly hosts, you his servants who do his will. Praise the Lord, all his works everywhere in his dominion. Praise the Lord, my soul.

Adoption Bible Stories

When God was speaking to me about adoption, it had never occurred to me that in the Bible, there were stories of children who had been adopted. Jeremiah 29:11 (NIV) says, "'For I know the plans I have for you,' declares the LORD, 'plans to prosper you and not to harm you, plans to give you hope and a future." God has a plan and purpose for every single person, and that plan is all about life, health, hope, safety, blessings, and looking forward to a glorious future. So whether you were adopted or not adopted, you have all been given the choice to be a child in the kingdom of God. Just as your earthly father assumed full responsibility for his/her adopted child, your Heavenly Father assumed responsibility for you. He loves you! He provided and equipped you with everything you'll ever need to live the abundant life chosen for you.

There are a few stories in the Bible pertaining to adoption, but I am only going to touch on three of them. The amazing outcome of each of these stories is God made a way for each of these children to influence their people and impact people all around them. God had a plan for each of these children, and it reflected hope for their generation and generations to follow. The children who were adopted were Moses, Esther, and Jesus.

Pharaoh's Daughter and Moses

Exodus Chapter 1 tells a story of a new king who reigned over Egypt. In verses 8–10 (NIV), it says:

> Then a new king, to whom Joseph meant nothing, came to power in Egypt. "Look," he said to his people, "the Israelites have become far too numerous for us. Come, we must deal shrewdly with them or they will become even more numerous and, if war breaks out, will join our enemies, fight against us and leave the country."

The king spoke with the midwives and told them while they were assisting the Hebrew women with childbirth that if a girl was born, she could live, but if a boy was born, they were to kill him. The midwives feared God and could not carry out this awful request. The Israelites continued to increase in number. The king was displeased and questioned the midwives. He did not like the fact they didn't listen to him, so he declared every baby boy to be thrown into the river (1–22).

Exodus chapter 2 tells of a Levite woman who conceived and gave birth to a baby boy. This woman knew her baby was special and kept him hidden for three months to protect him from the Egyptians. In verses 3–4 (NLT), it says:

> But when she could no longer hide him, she got a basket made of papyrus reeds and waterproofed it with tar and pitch. She put the baby in the basket and laid it among the reeds along the bank of the Nile River. The baby's sister then stood at a distance, watching to see what would happen to him.

That mother did not want to give up her baby. Due to the circumstances in which she had no control over, she did this to save and protect him. The baby's sister observed him in the river until he was noticed and retrieved from the water by the maid of Pharaoh's daughter. The princess noticed that this was a Hebrew baby, and at that time, the baby's sister appeared asking if she would like for her to find a Hebrew woman to nurse the baby. The sister retrieved the baby's mother, and she was able to care for and nurse her own baby until he became older. The Hebrew woman returned the child to Pharaoh's daughter, who then adopted him as her own and named him Moses (5–10).

Moses grew up as a prince in the house of Pharaoh's daughter. "Moses was given the best education in Egypt. He was a strong man and a powerful speaker" (Acts 7:22, CEV). When he was around forty years old, he decided to visit the children of Israel and observe their hard labor. That day, Moses was angered as he witnessed a Hebrew man being unjustly beaten by an Egyptian man. Regrettably, when Moses thought no one was looking, he killed the Egyptian and buried him in the sand. The moment in time changed his life forever. When Moses discovered that the Hebrews and Pharaoh knew what he had done, Moses fled to a land called Midian, where he chose to dwell. Years passed, and the king died in Egypt. The Israelites cried out to God, asking Him for help. God acknowledged their prayers and called Moses to return to Egypt to bring the Israelites out of slavery into a fertile and spacious land full of milk and honey (Exodus 3:8). God had a plan for Moses from the beginning of time, just as He has a plan for you. I encourage you to seek God and unite with the plan He has created for you.

Mordecai and Esther

The following story tells about a child who unfortunately lost both of her parents to death. It is found in Esther 2:5–7 (NLT).

> At that time there was a Jewish man in the fortress of Susa whose name was Mordecai son of Jair. He was from the tribe of Benjamin and was a descendant of Kish and Shimei. His family had been among those who, with King Jehoiachin of Judah, had been exiled from Jerusalem to Babylon by King Nebuchadnezzar. This man had a very beautiful and lovely young cousin, Hadassah, who was also called Esther. When her father and mother died, Mordecai adopted her into his family and raised her as his own daughter.

Mordecai was a godly man who loved Esther and raised her to the best of his ability during a time of challenging circumstances for his family. When Esther was a young woman, King Ahasuerus appointed commissioners in each province of his kingdom to gather all the beautiful young women and take them to his harem. The women were told that whoever pleased the king would be the next queen. Mordecai was devastated, as Esther was removed from her home and taken to live in the king's harem. Esther found favor and grace in the sight of King Ahasuerus of Persia. The king was attracted to Esther more than any other woman in the land and chose her to be his wife and crowned her queen (Esther 2:17).

One day while Mordecai was sitting at the king's gates, he overheard a plot to kill the king. He sent a message to the queen for her to tell the king about what was going to happen. Mordecai did not receive any recognition for the discovery of the plot to kill the king, but rather, Hamen, and he was promoted high priest to the king. Hamen was a man of pride who wanted everyone to bow down to him. Mordecai refused to bow down to Haman, and that irritated Hamen. Hamen found out Mordecai's people were the Jews, and he devised a plan to have all of them killed. Hamen manipulated the king into creating a decree that all Jews would be killed (Esther 3:1–15).

When Mordecai heard the decree, he fell at the king's gates desperately crying. When Queen Esther heard of this, she was disturbed. Esther 4:5 (BSB) says, "Esther summoned Hathach, one of the king's eunuchs appointed to her, and she dispatched him to Mordecai to learn what was troubling him and why." Mordecai told Hathach about the plot to kill all the Jews and gave him a copy of the written decree. Mordecai told Hathach to show the decree to Esther, "…urging her to approach the king, implore his favor, and plead before him for her people" (Esther 4:8, BSB). This made Esther nervous because she had never told the king that she was a Jew. Esther told Hathach to tell Mordecai:

> "All the royal officials and the people of the king's provinces know that one law applies to every man or woman who approaches the king in the inner court without being summoned—that he be put to death. Only if the king extends the gold scepter may that person live. But I have not been summoned to appear before the king for the past thirty days."
>
> — Esther 4:11 (BSB)

Through repeated conversations back and forth between Mordecai and Hathach, Mordecai informed Esther in 4:13–14 (BSB):

> "Do not imagine that because you are in the king's palace you alone will escape the fate of all the Jews. For if you remain silent at this time, relief and deliverance for the Jews will arise from another place, but you and your father's house will perish. And who knows if perhaps you have come to the kingdom for such a time as this?"

Esther agreed and asked Mordecai to have all the Jews in Susa fast for three days, and then she would go before the king. Queen Esther depended on God, and despite all obstacles, she approached the king. The king was happy to see her and stretched forth the golden scepter, asking her what she requested. God gave Esther wisdom and favor in how to inform the king of the decree to kill the Jews, and God saved her people.

In this story, Esther was adopted because both of her parents died. It was an unforeseen event, but God had a plan for Esther. He placed her in a home where her adoptive father loved, nurtured, and cared for her. Esther became a woman of great influence. God used her to spare the lives of the Jewish people and change their destiny.

Joseph and Jesus

This next story is about the birth of Jesus. I had never looked at this passage in scripture in regards to adoption, but did you know that Jesus was actually adopted and raised by an earthly father? God entrusted Joseph and Mary to raise His Son, Jesus, who would eventually become the Savior of the world. Matthew 1:18–21 (NLT) tells the following story:

> …Mary was engaged to be married to Joseph. But before the marriage took place, while she was still a virgin, she became pregnant through the power of the Holy Spirit. Joseph, to whom she was engaged, was a righteous man and did not want to disgrace her publicly, so he decided to break the engagement quietly.
>
> As he considered this, an angel of the Lord appeared to him in a dream. "Joseph, son of David," the angel said, "do not be afraid to take Mary as your wife. For the child within her was conceived by the Holy Spirit. And she will have a son, and you are to name him Jesus, for he will save his people from their sins."

It then goes on to say in verses 24–25 (NLT), "When Joseph woke up, he did as the angel of the Lord commanded and took Mary as his wife. But he did not have sexual relations with her until her son was born. And Joseph named him Jesus."

Jesus was born in Bethlehem of Judea during the reign of King Herod. There were three wise men who approached the king, asking him where the baby who would be king of the Jews was born. This troubled King Herod, and he wanted to seek out this baby. These wise men continued on their way in the search for this baby king. They followed the star in the sky until it rested over the location where they found Jesus with His mother. The wise men presented to Him gifts fit for a king, gold, frankincense, and myrrh. After the wise men left, an angel of the Lord showed up in another dream and told Joseph to move to Egypt, as King Herod was going to search for and destroy the child (Matthew 2:1–15).

Every time Jesus was in danger, an angel of the Lord would appear in a dream and tell Joseph what his next step would be. God, Joseph, and Mary worked together to raise Jesus. When Jesus was older and ready to be baptized, He went to the Jordan River to be baptized by John the Baptist, His cousin. In Matthew 3:16–17 (ESV), it says:

> And when Jesus was baptized, immediately he
> went up from the water, and behold, the heavens
> were opened to him, and he saw the Spirit of God
> descending like a dove and coming to rest on him;
> and behold, a voice from heaven said, "This is my
> beloved Son, with whom I am well pleased."

Jesus was then led by the Spirit into the wilderness to be tempted and fast for forty days. Afterward, Jesus started His ministry, selected His team of disciples, and began preaching and teaching about the kingdom of God, and healed all people who would have faith to receive. Jesus continued to seek His Heavenly Father and only did what He saw His Heavenly Father do (John 5:19–23).

God had a plan for Jesus. John 3:16–17 (NIV) says, "For God so loved the world that he gave his one and only Son, that whoever believes in him shall not perish but have eternal life. For God did not send his Son into the world to condemn the world, but to save the world through him." Jesus was brought to this earth to restore our relationship with our Heavenly Father. I would like to end this section and chapter with Colossians 1:15–20 (AMP):

> "He is the exact living image [the essential manifestation] of the unseen God [the visible representation of the invisible], the firstborn [the preeminent one, the sovereign, and the originator] of all creation. For by Him all things were created in heaven and on earth, [things] visible and invisible, whether thrones or dominions or rulers or authorities; all things were created *and* exist through Him [that is, by His activity] and for Him. And He Himself existed *and* is before all things, and in Him all things hold together. [His is the controlling, cohesive force of the universe.] He is also the head [the life-source and leader] of the body, the church; and He is the beginning, the firstborn from the dead, so that He Himself will occupy the first place [He will stand supreme and be preeminent] in everything. For it pleased the *Father* for all the fullness [of deity—the sum total of His essence, all His perfection, powers, and attributes] to dwell [permanently] in Him (the Son), and through [the intervention of] the Son to reconcile all things to Himself, making peace [with believers] through the blood of His cross; through Him, [I say,] whether things on earth or things in heaven."

CHAPTER 5

Sharing the Love
of the Father

When you hear or think of the word "father," what thoughts come to your mind? You may see a picture of your father, a friend's father, a man of great influence in your life, or some actor who played the role of a father in a movie or on television. Whomever you see in that picture has deposited an imprint on your heart. Let's take a look at a few vital roles a father plays in shaping and molding his children's lives:

- A father plays an important role in the family and in raising his children.

- He contributed to the uniqueness and design of the children's genetic makeup with characteristics that only came from the father.

- A father is known as the provider of the family. He enjoys being with his children and showers them with gifts because it gives him great joy.

- A father believes in disciplining his children. Of course, children think it's unfair, but it sets boundaries for the children and helps correct any defiant behaviors. Children learn respect and develop character, trust, security, and protection through their father's discipline.

- A father loves his children no matter how they act, what they do, or how they live because they are the very image of him and the representation of his life. A father understands that even though his child or children's behavior may hurt him, he still loves them. Though the child's behavior may not be acceptable, a father's love is from the heart and not determined by the behavior.

I love the example found in 1 Corinthians 13:4–8 (NIV). This would be a perfect example of a father's love for his children. It says:

> Love is patient, love is kind. It does not envy, it does not boast, it is not proud. It does not dishonor others, it is not self-seeking, it is not easily angered, it keeps no record of wrongs. Love does not delight in evil but rejoices with the truth. It always protects, always trusts, always hopes, always perseveres. Love never fails.

I realize that you may not have had a father portrayed in 1 Corinthians 13:4–8, but let's look at Matthew 7:11 (NASB): "So if you, *despite* being evil, know how to give good gifts to your children, how much more will your Father who is in heaven give good things to those who ask Him!" So, even if you had a sinful father, look back on his life and reflect on what he did for you.

Search your heart and find something that you can be grateful for. Proverbs 23:22 (ISV) says to "Listen to the one who fathered you…" and Exodus 20:12 (AMP) says, "Honor (respect, obey, care for) your father and your mother, so that your days may be prolonged in the land the LORD your God gives you."

I did not have a stable father-daughter relationship growing up. I know that my stepdad loved me even though he was abusive and drank all the time. He did take time for me. He understood me and the desires that I had in my life during my teen years. I know in my heart that he knew someday I would find out about my biological father. I am sure it probably hurt him when I desired to have a relationship with my biological father, who did not raise me. When I turned fifteen, my mother and stepdad divorced; however, I always remained in contact with him during my late teen years and young adult years. Before he died, he had accepted Jesus Christ into his heart. He had such excitement in his voice when I spoke with him and joy knowing that he was forgiven for all of the terrible things he had done in the past.

I am so thankful that my biological father came into my life. He introduced me to my Heavenly Father in a whole new level. I learned to seek God and intimately connect with Him through prayer, worship, and reading His Word. As our relationship grew stronger, God healed my broken heart and the hurtful wounds that had developed over the years. I was disowned by my friends and family and accused of being religious. They did not understand the peace and freedom I experienced in my relationship with God. While in His presence, He would shower me with love, kindness, and acceptance. I knew He was for me and not against me. I felt safe in His arms, knowing that my life was in His hands. I learned to trust again and had hope for a brighter future.

Whatever your experience was with your earthly father, know that you have a Heavenly Father who loves you. John 3:16–17 (NIV) says, "For God so loved the world that he gave his one and only Son, that whoever believes in him shall not perish but have eternal life. For God did not send his Son into the world to condemn the world, but to save the world through him." God loves you so much that He sacrificed His only Son to reap a harvest of sons and daughters through the salvation of Jesus Christ. When you choose to join the heavenly family, you are adopted into the kingdom of God and joint-heirs with Jesus Christ. Romans 8:17 (NIV) says, "Now if we are children, then we are heirs—heirs of God and co-heirs with Christ…"

God described a father's love by giving an example found in 1 John 4:7–12 (NIV). It says:

> Dear friends, let us love one another, for love comes from God. Everyone who loves has been born of God and knows God. Whoever does not love does not know God, because God is love. This is how God showed his love among us: He sent his one and only Son into the world that we might live through him. This is love: not that we loved God, but that he loved us and sent his Son as an atoning sacrifice for our sins. Dear friends, since God so loved us, we also ought to love one another. No one has ever seen God; but if we love one another, God lives in us and his love is made complete in us.

I would like to share a letter that describes the intimate love that our Heavenly Father has for us. The words that you are about to read come from the very heart of God. It is a compilation of paraphrased Bible verses from Genesis to Revelation that expresses the love of God in written form. He is the Father you have been looking for all your life. This is His love letter to you![7]

A Father's Love Letter

You may not know me, but I know everything about you. *Psalm 139:1*

I know when you sit down and when you rise up. *Psalm 139:2*

I am familiar with all your ways. *Psalm 139:3*

Even the very hairs on your head are numbered. *Matthew 10:29–31*

For you were made in my image. *Genesis 1:27*

In me you live and move and have your being. *Acts 17:28*

For you are my offspring. *Acts 17:28*

I knew you even before you were conceived. *Jeremiah 1:4–5*

I chose you when I planned creation. *Ephesians 1:11–12*

You were not a mistake, for all your days are written in my book. *Psalm 139:15–16*

I determined the exact time of your birth and where you would live. *Acts 17:26*

You are fearfully and wonderfully made. *Psalm 139:14*

---

7   You can also watch the corresponding video at https://www.youtube.com/watch?v=58hvHHmDISc.

I knit you together in your mother's womb. *Psalm 139:13*

And brought you forth on the day you were born. *Psalm 71:6*

I have been misrepresented by those who don't know me. *John 8:41–44*

I am not distant and angry, but am the complete expression of love. *1 John 4:16*

And it is my desire to lavish my love on you. *1 John 3:1*

Simply because you are my child and I am your Father. *1 John 3:1*

I offer you more than your earthly father ever could. *Matthew 7:11*

For I am the perfect father. *Matthew 5:48*

Every good gift that you receive comes from my hand. *James 1:17*

For I am your provider and I meet all your needs. *Matthew 6:31–33*

My plan for your future has always been filled with hope. *Jeremiah 29:11*

Because I love you with an everlasting love. *Jeremiah 31:3*

My thoughts toward you are countless as the sand on the seashore. *Psalm 139:17–18*

And I rejoice over you with singing. *Zephaniah 3:17*

I will never stop doing good to you. *Jeremiah 32:40*

For you are my treasured possession. *Exodus 19:5*

I desire to establish you with all my heart and all my soul. *Jeremiah 32:41*

And I want to show you great and marvelous things. *Jeremiah 33:3*

If you seek me with all your heart, you will find me. *Deuteronomy 4:29*

Delight in me and I will give you the desires of your heart. *Psalm 37:4*

For it is I who gave you those desires. *Philippians 2:13*

I am able to do more for you than you could possibly imagine. *Ephesians 3:20*

For I am your greatest encourager. *2 Thessalonians 2:16–17*

I am also the Father who comforts you in all your troubles. *2 Corinthians 1:3–4*

When you are brokenhearted, I am close to you. *Psalm 34:18*

As a shepherd carries a lamb, I have carried you close to my heart. *Isaiah 40:11*

One day I will wipe away every tear from your eyes. *Revelation 21:3–4*

And I'll take away all the pain you have suffered on this earth. *Revelation 21:3–4*

I am your Father, and I love you even as I love my son, Jesus. *John 17:23*

For in Jesus, my love for you is revealed. *John 17:26*

He is the exact representation of my being. *Hebrews 1:3*

He came to demonstrate that I am for you, not against you. *Romans 8:31*

And to tell you that I am not counting your sins. *2 Corinthians 5:18–19*

Jesus died so that you and I could be reconciled. *2 Corinthians 5:18–19*

His death was the ultimate expression of my love for you. *1 John 4:10*

I gave up everything I loved that I might gain your love. *Romans 8:31–32*

If you receive the gift of my son Jesus, you receive me. *1 John 2:23*

And nothing will ever separate you from my love again. *Romans 8:38–39*

Come home and I'll throw the biggest party heaven has ever seen. *Luke 15:7*

I have always been Father, and will always be Father. *Ephesians 3:14–15*

My question is… Will you be my child? *John 1:12–13*

I am waiting for you. *Luke 15:11–32*

Love Your Dad, Almighty God[8]

---

8   Father's Love Letter used by permission © 1999 Father Heart Communications. www.FathersLoveLetter.com.

CHAPTER 6

Family Choices—Eternity with the Father

I cannot write a book without giving you an opportunity to meet Jesus. As you read this book, I pray it stirred up a desire within your heart to live a life for God or rekindle the relationship you once had with Him. The first step to living a life for God is to make sure that you're a child of God.

The Bible says that all who call upon the name of the Lord shall be saved. Ephesians 2:8–9 (ESV) says, "For by grace you have been saved through faith. And this is not your own doing; it is the gift of God, not a result of works, so that no one may boast." John 3:16 (ESV) says, "For God so loved the world, that He gave His only Son, that whoever believes in Him should not perish but have eternal life." Romans 10:9–10 (NIV) says, "If you declare with your mouth, 'Jesus is Lord,' and believe in your heart that God raised Him from the dead, you will be saved. For it is with your heart that you believe and are justified, and it is with your mouth that you profess your faith and are saved."

Do You Desire to Live a Life for Jesus Christ?

The exciting part about being in the family of God is that you have a Father who loves and cherishes you. He made you in your mother's womb, and He knows every hair on your head. You are the apple of His eye, and He loved you so much that He sacrificed His one and only Son so your relationship with God could be restored. Through Jesus's death and resurrection, He provided you with a way back to the Heavenly Father.

A Commitment to Jesus Christ

If something were to happen to you today, where would you spend eternity? I have had the opportunity to lead many people to Jesus Christ and have heard people respond with, "I go to church," "I am the biggest contributor in the church," "I grew up in the church," "I do a lot of good things for people," and some have flat out said, "I am going to hell." My response to that would be, "Let's just fix that right now and clarify where you will spend eternity." So, today, if you have invited Jesus into your heart, then you have eternity for assurance. If you have never invited Jesus into your heart, pray this prayer, believe it, and receive it.

> Dear Heavenly Father,
> I come to You as a child who wants to make certain of where I spend eternity. I confess before You that I know that I don't live the best life and could use Your help. I confess that I have sin in my life, and I want to make my life right before You today.
> You said if we confess our sins before You, You would forgive us. So, right now, I say that I am sorry

for everything that I have done. Help me to get it right and allow me to have an opportunity to live right before You.

I believe that Your Word is true. You said if I speak with my mouth, "Jesus is Lord," and believe in my heart that God raised Jesus from the dead, I would be saved. So God, right now, I take the step in faith to believe that I am saved. You are my God.

Jesus is my Savior, and the Holy Spirit is here to help me walk as a child of God.

Thank You, God, for a second chance. Thank You that I am now a child of God and belong to the heavenly kingdom.

I pray in Jesus' name.

Congratulations! You just made the most important decision of your life. Welcome to the family of God. You are a child of God and now joint-heirs with Jesus Christ. Romans 8:17 (ESV) says, "…if children, then heirs—heirs of God, and joint-heirs with Christ…" Ask God for wisdom that He will guide you in all the affairs of your life. Trust in God so He can help turn your life around and provide you with a fresh new start in life. It is important to read the Bible and find a good church that teaches the Word of God. Your pastor will help you grow and mature in the Word of God, and he will teach you how to live your life for God.

If you just accepted Jesus Christ as your personal Lord and Savior, please send me an email and tell me your story. I am so excited for you and would love to hear how God is touching and changing your life. I have also included my website address so you can learn about my ministry, Living in the Light Women's

Ministry International, and check out other products available in the online store.

- *Email at:* livinginthelightwmi@gmail.com.
- *Website address:* livinginthelightwmi.com.

Scriptures to Encourage You in Your Walk with Jesus Christ

Now that you have decided to follow Jesus Christ, I want to leave you with some scriptures from the Bible in the Amplified Version. Read these scriptures out loud and declare them over your life. Let the Word of God sink in and transform your thought life. As we close out this chapter of the book, I want to share one final verse. Philippians 4:8–9 (NIV) says:

> Finally, brothers and sisters, whatever is true,
> whatever is noble, whatever is right, whatever is pure,
> whatever is lovely, whatever is admirable—if anything
> is excellent or praiseworthy—think about such
> things. Whatever you have learned or received or
> heard from me, or seen in me—put it into practice.
> And the God of peace will be with you.

Salvation Scriptures

Guide me in Your truth and teach me, For You are the God of my salvation; For You [and only You] I wait [expectantly] all the day long.

— Psalm 25:5

For God alone my soul *waits* in silence; From Him comes my salvation.

— Psalm 62:1

For God so [greatly] loved and dearly prized the world, that He [even] gave His [One and] only begotten Son, so that whoever believes and trusts in Him [as Savior] shall not perish, but have eternal life.

— John 3:16

And it shall be that whoever shall call upon the name of the Lord [invoking, adoring, and worshiping the Lord—Christ] shall be saved.

— Acts 2:21

And there is salvation in no one else; for there is no other name under heaven that has been given among people by which we must be saved [for God has provided the world no alternative for salvation].

— Acts 4:12

He then brought them out and asked, "Sirs, what must I do to be saved?" They replied, "Believe in the Lord Jesus, and you will be saved—you and your household."

— Acts 16:30–31 (NIV)

I am not ashamed of the gospel, for it is the power of God for salvation [from His wrath and punishment] to everyone who believes [in Christ as Savior], to the Jew first and also to the Greek.

— Romans 1:16

If you declare with your mouth, "Jesus is Lord," and believe in your heart that God raised Him from the dead, you will be saved. For it is with your heart that you believe and are justified, and it is with your mouth that you profess your faith and are saved.

— Romans 10:9–10 (NIV)

For "whoever calls on the name of the Lord [in prayer] will be saved."

— Romans 10:13

Therefore, if anyone is in Christ, the new creation has come: The old has gone, the new is here!

— Second Corinthians 5:17 (NIV)

From My Heart to Yours

God made Him who had no sin to be sin for us, so that in Him we might become the righteousness of God.

— Second Corinthians 5:21 (NIV)

For it is by grace you have been saved, through faith—and this is not from yourselves, it is the gift of God—not by works, so that no one can boast.

— Ephesians 2:8–9 (NIV)

But [we are different, because] our citizenship is in heaven. And from there we eagerly await [the coming of] the Savior, the Lord Jesus Christ.

— Philippians 3:20

This is good, and pleases God our Savior, who wants all people to be saved and to come to a knowledge of the truth.

— First Timothy 2:3–4 (NIV)

But you are a chosen people, a royal priesthood, a holy nation, God's special possession, that you may declare the praises of Him who called you out of darkness into his wonderful light.

— First Peter 2:9 (NIV)

My dear children, I write this to you so that you will not sin. But if anybody does sin, we have an advocate with the Father—Jesus Christ, the Righteous One. He is the atoning sacrifice for our sins, and not only for ours but also for the sins of the whole world.

— First John 2:1–2 (NIV)

"Behold, I stand at the door [of the church] and *continually* knock. If anyone hears My voice and opens the door, I will come in and eat with him (restore him), and he with Me."

— Revelation 3:20

SPECIAL ADDITION

What you are about to read on the next few pages exhibits the love an earthly father has for his children and, in return, the respect, appreciation, and influence he has made in his children. May these love letters touch your heart and impact your life.

A Love Letter to Our Children from Their Father
by Leslie Elliott

FROM A FATHER'S HEART TO HIS CHILDREN

You, my child:

You are the completion of love within my heart and innermost being.

There is nothing that is upright before God that I wouldn't do or sacrifice in order to provide for you, even if it meant giving up life itself.

Personal sacrifice is not a loss but rather an expression of the height, breadth, and depth of my love for you. Possessions, time, and talent can all be measured. The love I feel for you…never-ending.

I fondly recall the conversations we have had, where we were, the tears that both of us shed…they are precious to me.

I have felt the weight of your heart during challenging times and have delighted in the midst of your success, for you have recognized that failure is not a destination but merely hurdles on your road to fulfilling your destiny. The hurdles did not hurt you; they were reminders that sacrifices have to be made to achieve your goals.

Life begins and ends with love. Let love become your end goal! Our Heavenly Father is the author of love. God is love. Without love, we have nothing worthy of striving for. It is this love that compels us to sacrifice our lives for another. Love is not a result of sacrifice but rather sacrifice the result of love.

I pray that you make the scriptures found in 1 Corinthians 13th chapter indelibly written upon your heart and ask God for His grace to live this out in your lives.

I love you, children.

I always have.

I always will.

…No matter what!

With love, Dad

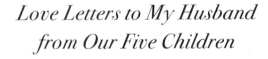

Love Letters to My Husband from Our Five Children

THE MAN I AM TODAY

I am the man I am today
Because of my dad.
He raised and cared for me,

Made God and church a priority,
Taught me right from wrong.
I always felt I belonged.
He skipped meals for me,
Worked long hours for me,
Went back to school to provide a better life for me.

We didn't always agree,
But he was always there for me,
Not just for homework while in school
But also helping me move to new cities,
Getting married, covering some bills,
In his free time taught me life skills,
How to use various tools;
These benefit me to this day.

And even now, is sound counsel.
A man of few words
Loves a good joke.
You can feel the love being with him,
That he really cares.
My dad is a good dad.
He's led by example.
He's one in a million,
And I wouldn't have it any other way.

I have my own family now,
And looking to my own future,
Having a great example to follow,
I want to do the same for those that come after me
To show them how to be successful in life,

A good work ethic, to work hard,
To value learning and bettering yourself,
To never give up, to live.

I love you, Dad.

—Brandon

Dad,

I don't know how to put into words the appreciation I feel towards my dad and the example he has proven to us in how to conduct ourselves while growing up.

My dad is not one to talk much; he mainly demonstrates his belief through actions. Actions that many will never know of, as they are conducted silently and without pretense or expectation of anything in return.

I will forever be grateful for his belief in me and support of what all others have politely called crazy endeavors. Many don't go after their dreams and aspirations due to the lack of belief from their dad or resulting insecurities. I cannot thank him enough for not including us in that majority and showing us through conduct how we are to treat and believe in others.

—Joshua

Dad,

I'm your one and only little girl out of five children. I remember while growing up, every time I was proud of something that I had done, I would say, "Watch me, Daddy." I would look back to see if you were watching, and you were.

You made time for me, and we went on father and daughter date nights. You would spend the time showing me how a daughter should truly be treated as a woman. You have always been there for me and supported me. There were times in my life when my choices caused me to learn life experiences on my own, but even at that time, you were still there to help me.

I am older now, with two daughters of my own; however, I still call you all the time for guidance. You are the smartest man I know, and you are so wise. I am thankful that you were there for the birth of both my daughters, and when I was going through some really rough patches in my life, you set an example for my daughters as well. For several years, you were their father figure, and now that I look back, I cannot thank you enough for what you have done. I can't imagine life without you, nor do I want to. You are everything to me and my girls.

The most beautiful thing I can say to this day is your marriage to Mom. The way you honor her, encourage her, and strengthen her. You both respect one another, and because I have seen the life that you give one another, I have prayed for several years that I could have the same kind of relationship. God has finally given this man to me, and I can't wait for you to walk me down the aisle to marry him. With that being said, it will be one of the hardest things I do as I leave you and join my future husband in marriage. It brings tears to my eyes just writing this passage to honor you. A part of me will be given to my future husband, but I would not have any of this without you encouraging me and molding me to what I am today.

Thank you for showing me how a young lady should behave. Thank you for showing me that God is the only way, and through hard times and easy times alike, I still must rely and depend on Him. I truly have the best father that was ever created, and I thank God every day He chose me to be your daughter.

—Keirsha

Dad,

To begin with, you are my hero and my role model. I am super grateful that I have you as my dad. No matter the circumstances, and we both work in crazy fields, I know I can always count on you. You have raised me to never give up on anything, no matter how hard it can be at times. You have taught me how to raise a family. You will always be my dad. Thank you for never giving up on me. I love you, Dad!

—Nathaniel

A SACRED TRUST

When a man becomes a father, having a child of his own,
He's given a trust like none other;
It's his but not his alone.

Life and love; Jehovah is the one true source
Given sure direction that his child follows the wisest course.

A sacred trust—given,
A precious life—in his hands
To instruct the child in all God's commands.

All these words God has given
…my father, in turn, inculcates these in us.
Whether in rising or while at rest,
In years to come, may we remember,
May we be faithful, May we be blessed.

My earthly father has done just that.

—Jonathan

BIBLIOGRAPHY

Ballenger, Mark. What Is the Difference Between Condemnation and Conviction? Last modified August 2, 2017. https://applygodsword.com/what-is-the-difference-between-condemnation-and-conviction.

Children's Hospital Colorado. "What Every Child Needs." 2021. https://www.childrenscolorado.org/conditions-and-advice/parenting/parenting-articles/what-children-need.

Denison, Jason. "Names of God (4K Version)." February 13, 2018. YouTube video, 3:36. https://www.youtube.com/watch?v=oP25kCPocwg.

Dictionary.com. Accessed 2021. https://www.dictionary.com.

Elliott, B. Personal letter used by permission. 2021.

Elliott, J. A. Personal letter used by permission. 2021.

Elliott, J. D. Personal letter used by permission. 2021.

Elliott, K. Personal letter used by permission. 2021.

Elliott, L. Personal love letter used by permission. 2021.

Elliott, N. Personal letter used by permission. 2021.

Father's Love Letter. Father Heart Communications, 1999. www.FathersLoveLetter.com. Used by permission.

Free Bible Lessons. "The Trinity." Last modified 2021. https://freebiblelessons.net/object-lessons/trinity.

Peterson, Eugene H. *The Holy Bible*, The Message (MSG). Accessed June 22, 2021. https://www.biblegateway.com.

The Bible App. *The Holy Bible*, Amplified Version (AMP). 2008–2019. https://www.bible.com.

The Holy Bible, Berean Study Bible. 2004–2020. https://bible.com.

The Holy Bible, Contemporary English Version. 2004–2020. https://bible.com.

The Holy Bible, English Standard Version (ESV). 2004–2020. https://bible.com.

The Holy Bible, New International Version (NIV). 2004–2020. https://bible.com.

The Holy Bible, New Living Translation Version (NLT). 2004–2020. https://bible.com.

The Holy Bible, New King James Version (NKJV). 2004–2020. https://bible.com.

THELAW.com Dictionary. "Adoption." 1995–2015. https://dictionary.thelaw.com/adoption.

ABOUT THE AUTHOR

Connie Elliott and her husband, Leslie, live in Sebastian, Florida, and have been married for over thirty-four years. They have five grown children and four grandchildren. They have spent their married years investing in their family, setting an example of God's unfailing love, and helping their children to stay strong in their faith and walk in God. One thing we know for sure is that God is always with us and we are never alone.

God's Word says that He gives us the desires of our hearts. Connie has desired to write books for God and encourage people to press into the call of God placed on their lives. She desires that when this book is read, it gives you hope, faith, and encouragement in the possibilities of God, knowing in your heart that with God, all things are possible. Just as the Holy Spirit gave the disciples in the New Testament the ability to write letters, it is also Connie's desire to write encouraging words that will give inspiration to all who read her books.

It is Connie's prayer that you continue growing in God's Word and share the goodness of God in your life with others. We must remember to never give up on God. The one scripture that Connie continually stands on in her life is Galatians 6:9 (ESV). It says, "And let us not grow weary of doing good, for in due season we will reap, if we do not give up." Don't give up! You may want to but don't. In your weakest moments, speak the Word. Speak what you want, not what you have. You will be amazed at how God will turn situations around as you continually look to Him and place your trust in His goodness and unfailing love.

OTHER PRODUCT RESOURCES

Connie Elliott is the founder, president, and CEO of Living in the Light Women's Ministry International, LLC, located in Sebastian, Florida. She developed Scripture Script (SSx), which includes nine different products to assist the body of believers to stand firm on the Word of God.

Connie is also the author of *Be Encouraged* and *Inspirational Messages for Daily Encouragement.* They are available through Trilogy Christian Publishing, Amazon, Barnes and Noble, Books a Million, Walmart, Target, etc., and available in electronic versions.

If you would like to learn more about this ministry, request a speaking opportunity, or purchase one of the SSx product lines, visit the online store at livinginthelightwmi.com, or you may contact by email at livinginthelightwmi@gmail.com. See the following pages for products available for purchase.

Be Encouraged

You have been invited to a party prepared just for you. Pull up a chair and sit at the table. It is time to be encouraged and refreshed in the Word of God.

Be Encouraged is an uplifting book that will inspire you to walk with God as you never have before. You will learn how you can depend and rely on the Holy Spirit in every aspect of your life. Personal life stories and examples are shared to provide hope and encouragement in your life, marriage, family, and career. You will learn about how a man and woman can perform optimally in marriage by looking at the Proverbs 31 woman and the Ephesians 5 man. Whether single or married, this book will inspire you to live a life as a virtuous woman or a man of integrity. *Be Encouraged* will motivate you to seek God in a whole new level for your life. When you start reading this book, it will be one you won't want to put down!

Inspirational Messages for Daily Encouragement

May the inspiration of God's beauty speak to your heart and impact your life!

Inspirational Messages for Daily Encouragement will inspire and encourage you to walk out your faith in God with assurance, boldness, and confidence. You will visually see the beauty of God's creation combined with the written Word of God. You will be guided through captivating and inspirational messages to help you grow and mature in your walk with God. Additionally, you will read personal testimonies from real people who held onto the promises of God's Word until they achieved victory in their life and over their situations. You will also read stories from the Bible to strengthen your faith and give you hope.

Scripture Script (SSx)

God spoke to Connie on April 25, 2019, to make a container of life in which people would be able to stand on God's Word. Scripture Script (SSx) was designed and developed to get the Word of God into the body of Christ for believers to understand the significance in reading and meditating on God's Word. Proverbs 4:20–22 (KJV) says, "My son, attend to my words; incline thine ear unto my sayings. Let them not depart from thine eyes; keep them in the midst of thine heart. For they are life unto those that find them, and health to all their flesh."

You might ask, "Why SSx?" God's Word tells us to call those things which be not as though they were (Romans 4:17). The Word also tells us to declare the end from the beginning (Isaiah 46:10). We must speak what we want in our lives. God created the universe with His words, and He has given us the same ability for our lives. The Bible says in Proverbs 18 that death and life are in the power of the tongue, and they that love it shall eat the fruit thereof. It is imperative to understand that our words have power. Therefore, to live a life of health, healing, and victory, we must speak and declare the Word to see the manifestation in our lives. It is God's desire that you walk in the victory that you were given when Jesus died on the cross for our redemption.

Each SSx product has a thirty-day supply of scriptures to be read and meditated on throughout the day. Each container has its own personalized medication instruction sheet to replicate what a medical prescription bottle would have. This is to increase people's awareness that God's Word is medicine and produces life and healing to them that speak the Word of God over their lives. When you purchase the product, you will find the instruction sheet fastened to the container of life. To order any of the following nine different products, go to https://www.livinginthelightwmi.com/scripture-script-ssx. See the example below of SSx Logo and Wisdom SSx.

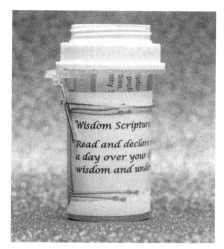

- Healing Scripture Script

- Peace Scripture Script

- Joy Scripture Script

- Wisdom Scripture Script

- Faith Scripture Script

- Prosperity Scripture Script

- Hope Scripture Script

- Encouragement Scripture Script

- Multivitamin Scripture Script